Blogging for Prof

I0011197

The Beginner's Guide to Passive Income with Blogging

Table of Contents

Introduction

Choosing a Profitable Niche

Benefits of a Custom Domain

Marketing Your Blog

Search Engine Optimization (SEO) Tactics

Say Goodbye to Writer's Block

Work Smarter, Not Harder

Dangerous Blogging Mistakes to Avoid

Monetization Tactics

Closing Words

Introduction

Blogging can change your life. It certainly has the potential to generate a considerable stream of passive income – if you know what to write about and how to gather an audience. This eBook teaches you just that as well as the fundamentals every aspiring blogger needs to learn about. In this step by step guide, everything from choosing your niche and marketing your blog to SEO tactics and monetization is extensively covered. If you have been raring to jump into the land of blogging but have hesitated for whatever reason, then this is the guide for you to use and finally take action. While the eBook does not go into the specifics on setting up a blog per se, it does teach all the factors that revolves around it once it has already been setup. Anyone can start a blog and earn a decent amount of revenue from it. Create content that matters (select a popular niche) and you will already be on the right track. As long as the factors analyzed in this book fall nicely into place, there is not a reason that you should not see at least some success.

At the risk of appearing to sugarcoat everything, a few words of honesty regarding the implications of blogging must be disclosed. Like any other method of passive income, this is not an easy journey by any means and will obviously require effort and persistency on your part. You must enjoy writing and creating content, or it will be difficult for you to do this effectively and you will likely be discouraged and give up. Furthermore, you must establish connections with other bloggers, especially when you are new. Every successful blogger naturally builds a Rolodex of contacts and for good reasoning. This will be expounded upon under the chapter **Marketing Your Blog.**

10 Reasons Why You Should Blog

With the compulsory words of realism out of the way, let us take a look at some of the more compelling reasons on why you should start a blog today.

1. **Anyone can start a blog.** Yes, that means you. If you are reading this, it is extremely likely that you already have the simple skills needed to bootstrap a blog.
2. **Establish yourself as an expert.** A blog is the place to position yourself as a well-respected expert in your niche. The more beneficial your viewers see you and the more problems you solve, the more they will return to your blog.
3. **Become more knowledgeable.** Researching the facts in your niche to stay up to date is an ineluctable responsibility of running a blog. You will continually gain information in the niche at your disposal.
4. **Sharpen your writing skills.** It does not matter if you are not a great writer. As long as you remain consistent in your blogging, your ability to write proficiently will continue to improve.
5. **Voice yourself.** Do you have something to say about a product in the niche you are passionate about? Is there something you disagree with? Blog about it so that you can let others know!
6. **Gain clients.** As your blog gradually builds up traffic, it is only inevitable that you begin to build a list of contacts that could one day serve to be potentially invaluable assets.
7. **Differentiate yourself.** How many people actually contribute to the Internet? According to the 1% rule, only 1% of Internet users are actively contributing to the web. The other 99% continue to do nothing but consume content. By contributing to the Internet ecosystem, you are standing out from the 99% of Internet users that do not create content.

8. **Learn to organize yourself.** Blogging compels you to organize and articulate your thoughts. The more you do this, the better you become at it.
9. **Become more confident.** The more traffic you gain, the more weight your opinions have. Blogging will help you quickly realize that your thoughts do matter and that people do care about what you have to say.
10. **Earn an income.** We finally highlight the driving incentive on why internet users begin blogging in the first place: monetization. Blogging has the potential to transcend from a hobby that produces a side income to something that could replace a day job!

If the above factors are not incentive enough for you to at least consider blogging, then what more do you want? Even with money out of the picture, there are still significant benefits to blogging in your spare time. Of course, this is all easier said than done, which is why this eBook was written. Unless you are writing purely for your own enjoyment, the very first step to blogging is choosing a profitable niche – a market that is not too broad and certainly not too saturated. This will be thoroughly explored in the following chapter: **Choosing a Profitable Niche**.

Choosing a Profitable Niche

Ideally, everyone wants to write what they are most passionate about. In optimal circumstances, something that one is passionate about will have a market and is not too saturated. Unfortunately, this does not always prove to be true. Unless money is not the driving factor for you, however, compromises must be made. If someone's passionate hobby entails something that is obscure or far too popular, it is not going to be a viable niche and that passion cannot be followed. When certain factors prevent the hobby from transcending into a profitable niche, one should look towards researching profitable niches that are at least moderately interesting to that person.

Assuming that you are serious about blogging, you will invest an inordinate amount of time in that niche over the coming years. This is the reason why bloggers cannot simply start writing about whatever niche they please and hope that traffic begins trickling in. If only a few hundred people are searching for keywords relevant to your niche, expect to receive even less monthly visitors than that. There has to be a demand for what is being written, or else the blog will never be successful. It is never possible to know for sure that what you write will be popular, but the following methods for choosing a profitable niche will undoubtedly guide you in making a decision.

Research Hot Keywords

Researching hot keywords entails utilizing the free Google AdWords Keyword Tool to find out what keywords the audience in any given niche is predominately searching for. If you do not already have an AdWords account, create a new one and sign in. This tool provides an ample amount of insightful data pertaining to statistics such as monthly search volume, keyword ideas, competition, etc. A monthly search volume that is in the thousands is a good indicator that there is potential profit to be made in that niche. However, be leery of oversaturated markets, which are generally characterized by excessively high monthly search volumes. If the keyword phrase you searched for returns keyword variations with similar traffic levels, this is a dead giveaway that many others are pursuing those same keyword variations. Because the tool does have its flaws and is not exactly pinpoint accurate, one should not solely rely on this tool when it comes to selecting a niche. Consider experimenting with similar tools to procure optimum results. In any case, such research tools should most certainly be used in conjunction with the following methods in an attempt to corroborate their potential for profitability.

Research Niche Market Trends

Garnering data for the monthly search volume of your niche keywords is great, but it is essential to see what direction that niche market has been heading. While a niche market may ostensibly seem worthy of investing in with a healthy monthly search volume based on the Keyword Tool, its monthly search volume could be on a downward trend overall. To get a better idea of whether the potential niche market is growing or declining, it is highly recommended to use Google Trends. Unlike the previous method, this tool does not require an account. Simply search your niche's relevant keywords and the tool will return the keywords' trending search volume over the past few years as well as its demographics. When considering a niche for a long term business, one should aim for a market that is growing or somewhat stable at the very least. The declining of a niche is clearly a dead giveaway to avoid jumping into that niche.

Assess Your Strengths

While it is true that a niche should not be solely fueled by passion, it certainly cannot hurt to assess one's skills and strengths. For all we may know, any one of those skills may be the foundation for quite the profitable niche to blog about. Assess yourself and consider where your strengths lie. Perhaps you are passionate in a particular sport and would like to blog about the sport's intricacies and/or its relevant news. Maybe you are a video game fanatic and would like to produce gaming related posts along with reviews. Regardless of where the strengths lie, the next step is drilling down the skill/interest to a niche and researching its potential for profit. If such a niche does not appear to be worthwhile investing your time in, consider an alternative niche under the same topic or interest. For a niche of your interest to be profitable, it must have low competition and be able to be monetized through products/services or be popular enough to place advertisements. Monetizing your blog will be perused under the **Monetization Tactics** chapter.

Consider the Problems You Can Solve

Brainstorm common issues that frustrate the general population and how you can create value by solving their problems. Some like to refer to this as a "problem niche" or a "desperate niche." If you are knowledgeable about a confusing niche or have an interest in learning about one, then this is the perfect opportunity to blog about the said niche. If there is anything that you are in the habit of helping people with, then consider researching the profitability of such a niche. It would also be the most auspicious opening to simultaneously help people while earning an income. Because people are willing to spend money to resolve their problems by any means, deploying such a tactic is often a profitable source of revenue. However, it should be noted that the blogger should at least have an inclination towards the niche, or boredom and abandonment of the blog will likely ensue. Furthermore, do ensure that your content offers the value that it should, or you will likely not procure the results you most desire in the long run.

View Popular Blogs/Books

Simply viewing what works is quite the conducive method for sparking niche ideas of your own. Take a look at some of the most popular blogs/books out there with a quick search online. When it comes to the most successful blogs, they provide great examples of what a blog should be modelled after. Consider observing some of the shared qualities of the said blogs, as it is these shared qualities that make them successful in the first place. When searching for the best-selling books, Amazon is the optimal location to start. This offers a convenient, accurate indication of what people are currently interested in reading about. Take note of what blogs/books interest you, as they could serve to be the foundation for a potentially profitable niche. This is because you must be able to see yourself writing about the topic 12 months from now, lest you frequently succumb to writer's block. Of course, simply viewing a list of successful blogs/books is not enough information to conjecture whether any niche in particular will be profitable, but it does provide a good start.

Benefits of a Custom Domain

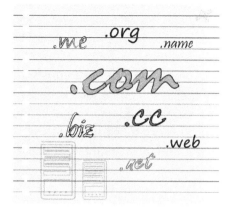

       While it does cost money on a recurring basis to host a custom domain, the benefits massively outweigh its fees as well as the alternative associated with selecting a subdomain. Many novice bloggers prefer to begin with a subdomain such as blogspot.com or wordpress.com because they are free, but this would actually be a dire mistake. It insinuates to the readers that the blogger is not treating the blog as a serious business. While one would presume that choosing a free subdomain is an ostensibly safe route, it is not conducive towards the blog's long term health. For example, if a blogger using a free subdomain suddenly becomes interested in purchasing and migrating to a custom domain, that custom domain (as well as .org and .net) name may have already been taken by then. That is a headache in itself, as the blogger then has to toil in rebranding the blog from square one. For those who are still on the fence of deciding between a custom domain and a subdomain, here are just a few of the reaped benefits that come with paying for the former.

Build Brand Name

       One of the immediate benefits of hosting a custom domain is the reinforcement of your brand name. The reason for this would be the use of a short custom domain, such as .com or .org, rather than a lengthy subdomain with blogspot.com or wordpress.com. Use of a custom domain also shifts the focus on the domain name rather than what would be a conspicuous subdomain. A custom domain also helps solidifies a more professional atmosphere and bolsters the viewer's impression of an authentic blog. As a result, viewers are much more likely to remember the website and perhaps return to it in the future. Combine this with a favicon, a logo, and a banner to secure maximum branding power. In short, a custom domain results in increased branding power. A more prominent brand name leads to a boost in viewer memorability and consequently more traffic. More traffic ultimately leads to increased income – all thanks to your initial investment in a custom domain.

Advertising Benefits

Most reputable advertisers will approve a custom domain much more seamlessly than they ever would with a blog using a subdomain. Many advertising companies are in the habit of rejecting subdomains, because they do not take such blogs seriously. Another reason for their propensity is because it indicates that you are able/willing to spend money on your business. This ties back to the credibility factor that a custom domain establishes. Sure, you save a little money by forgoing the custom domain, but this is an unmistakable opportunity cost that will only result in further loss of potential income.

Contact Email with Your Domain

Choosing a subdomain does not offer this option and leaves the blogger with no choice but to use a Yahoo, Gmail, or Outlook email for contact purposes – further accentuating a rather amateur atmosphere. Having a professional email with your domain name can go a long way, which is yet another compelling reason one should invest in a custom domain. This is because fortunately, another perk that comes with paying for a custom domain is the ability to use your custom domain with your email address. This would look similar to example@yourdomain.com.

Doing so further enhances your blog's professional demeanor as well as its authenticity at no additional cost. While some services do cost a monthly fee for use of an email with a custom domain, there are certainly a plethora of free options out there, contrary to what some may believe. A simple search for "free email services custom domain" would suffice.

Lasting Power

When you register your blog with a custom domain, you can rest assured that the blog will not be going anywhere anytime soon. As long as the subscription is continuously paid, the domain is yours to keep. This is not the case with subdomains, as there is always that chance that the blog could be taken down for whatever reason. While such cases are rare, they do occur regardless and a blogger does not deserve to be leery of the possibility of suspension. Choosing a custom domain will provide the peace of mind that you deserve so that your efforts can be better focused on more pertinent matters.

Establish Credibility

Naturally, blogs with a custom domain tend to be more respected than their subdomain counterparts. Therefore, it is easier to accrue credibility and respect with a custom domain than a blog sporting the glaring blogspot.com. This is because people generally hold an unfavorable impression of blogs with a subdomain. Why handicap yourself with such a limitation when it is difficult enough as it is to penetrate the blogging business? The reader typically presumes that the blogger is a free resource user and is not interested in following a person of that nature. Most people often regard .com and .org domains with higher value and consequently place more emphasis on them. While it is easy to presume that a blog with a subdomain is a 1-person team, it is also easy to view custom domain blogs as commercial websites ran by a group of people – further underlining the notion that the blog is significant in some way. A custom domain in itself does not establish the blog's authority, but it is certainly one of the driving factors.

Affordability

Another reason a blogger should consider a custom domain despite its recurring fees is the fact that it is extremely affordable – especially when purchased in conjunction with discount coupons. Think of it as an investment: Your long term return will be exponentially higher than if you were to have simply registered your blog with a subdomain. If you can afford to purchase a custom domain, then do so! Considering that this is an investment in a blogging business, such cheap prices should not be a deterrent anyways. If anything, the recurrent fees are but a small price to pay for the innumerable short and long term benefits it presents. It should therefore be concluded that there is most likely no excuse for a blogger to not purchase a custom domain.

Simplicity

To sum it all up, a custom domain is simpler than a subdomain. For example, compare the unique "www.myblog.com" as opposed to the generic "www.myblog.blogspot.com." Every time someone has to type the ".blogspot" after your domain name, it takes away from the professional quality of your blog. The former is simply more memorable and authentic, and people will take your blog more seriously. In any case, it appears much more visually appealing than the latter and will be more influential wherever the web address is seen. After reading this chapter, one thing should be clear by now: You need to stake your claim before someone else does. Do it now, before you end up regretting your hesitance.

Marketing Your Blog

This is the moment you have been waiting for. After finally choosing your niche and setting up the website for your blog, you now await the coveted readers that bloggers have long sought after. Many novice bloggers' initial enthusiasm inevitably begins to wane after seeing a lack of traffic. While it would be nice to simply upload blog post after blog post and gradually build your audience, neglecting the basic marketing tactics will unfortunately leave you at quite the disadvantage. With so many blogs seemingly sprouting up out of nowhere these days with abundant amounts of free information, it can be difficult to differentiate yourself from bloggers just like you. Implementing the following tips, however, will help ensure that your blog receives more traffic than the alternative of not utilizing them at all. Ultimately, it is the building of an online presence that will be most conducive towards your success.

Participate in Relevant Forums

Regularly contributing in forums pertinent to your niche is a great method of building your online presence as a prominent blogger. Do not tarnish your reputation by promoting yourself through spam-like methods; instead, it would be most conducive for you to be legitimately helpful and genuinely participate. By establishing yourself as a respected member of the forum's community, members will be much more likely to take you at face value. That is, members of the community will not suspect that the only reason you are even a member of the forums is to promote your blog. Different forums will stipulate different rules regarding self-promotion, so do be sure to become aware of them lest your account ends up banned.

Participate in Other Blogs

This is similar to the previously mentioned point in which you participate in relevant forums. Consider contributing thoughtful comments on blogs related to yours. Do not simply post cookie-cutter comments such as "Great blog! I really enjoyed reading this post" and include a link to your blog. This is patently seen as a desperate, spam-like attempt to market your blog. Rather, strive to make a real effort in joining the communities' discussions and lending your opinion as well as insightful feedback that can potentially benefit the blogger and readers. If you can do this, then you have surely earned the justification to briefly include a back link to one of your relevant blog posts. As a side note, it would be most effective to employ this strategy on the more popular blogs. After all, you would not want your valuable feedback to be for nothing on dead blogs.

Utilize Social Media

Never underestimate the power of social media, as it has the potential to significantly boost your exposure. Social networking has experienced tremendous expansion over the years and should be taken advantage of. Every successful blogger has prominence in the social media world, so it would be a good idea to emulate this. Of course, usage of social media accounts requires you to at least occasionally update your accounts to reap the maximum benefits. Every post you make on your blog should be updated on all your social media accounts to ensure that your readers know about it. By creating social networking accounts, this provides you with the opportunity to connect with potential readers that may have never known about your blog otherwise.

Create a Newsletter

Creating an email list should never be neglected, as most popular blogs incorporate this to remind readers that they exist. When someone signs up for your newsletter, that person is telling you that he or she wants to receive updates such as when you produce a new blog post. By giving your readers the option to sign up for your newsletter, you are making it easier for them to not only remember your blog but to tell their friends about it as well. Forget retaining your current audience: A newsletter can and will reach new demographics. This is because your more enthusiastic readers are apt to forward one of your emails to their friends. What about your less enthusiastic (casual) readers? They can likely be persuaded to join your email list by offering an incentive to sign up for your newsletter. Perhaps you are questioning the type of incentive you could possibly offer. Most bloggers opt to write a short eBook on something pertaining to their blogs and offer it for free to those who sign up for your newsletter.

Stay Consistent

Some bloggers will be ostensibly unwavering in their commitment to post on a fixed schedule and then randomly leave the blog without posting for weeks or even months on end. While consistency should be obvious, its importance cannot be stressed enough in order to keep the momentum of your blog going. Neglecting your blog whenever you feel like it will leave your readers wondering where you went. This is deleterious to the reputation of your blog including your own as a blogger. Readers would likely forget that your blog exists, and you can forget about the newsletter. Do not be surprised if readers begin unsubscribing to your email list, as they would have no longer have a reason to stick around. Stay consistent so your readers will see that you are serious and most importantly, reliable.

Incorporate Images

We are all visual creatures by nature, and the sparing use of images in your blog posts will liven up your blog while making your articles all the more pleasant to read. Of course, one should stray from using images found on Google to avoid committing copyright infringement. Your first thought may be the incorporation of free stock images, but one should be careful here. It is more convenient and time-saving to use stock images, but you should ensure that your competitors are not using them as well. This is because some readers will inevitably notice the same images being used and may single you out as trite or lazy. If many other blogs are using those stock images, it would be a better idea to create an image of your own: a conglomerate of public domain/stock photos perhaps. Creating your own image is the preferred method, but a stock photo is not a bad alternative if it is not already being excessively used.

Guest Posting

Rather than writing content for your own blog, consider writing content for *other* people's blogs. This may appear to be time-consuming and a waste of effort at first thought, but this can actually be highly beneficial for your blog. If you have the opportunity to guest post for a blog with copious visitors, take it. Doing so will attract interest to your blog, especially when the blog is relevant to your niche. If the blog is well known enough, you may wind up receiving referral traffic from that blog for months to come at the very least. This is because you will have the chance to include a link back to your own website on your guest post, also known as a backlink. Backlinks will be explained in the upcoming chapter: **Search Engine Optimization (SEO) Tactics**.

Search Engine Optimization (SEO) Tactics

Search Engine Optimization

Now we get into the nitty-gritty of blogging: search engine optimization. If you think you will be able to slide by as a blogger without learning about at least the basics of SEO tactics, you are going to have a bad time. In the most fundamental terms, search engine optimization is the visibility of your website in the organic search results of search engines – the visibility of which is affected by factors such as backlinks, domain age, traffic, etc. SEO also ties back to one of the benefits of having a custom domain, as Google does not favor subdomains or free blogs. If you have read this far and still are not convinced to opt for a custom domain, you may want to reconsider after reading this chapter and the importance of SEO. You do not have to be an SEO wizard by any means, but these are just a few SEO tactics a blogger should keep in mind for the sake of driving traffic to the blog.

Have a Custom Domain

You can tack this on as another benefit to having a custom domain: search engine optimization. There is some SEO research that suggests that having a custom domain will cause your blog to rank higher than if you were to opt for a subdomain. The increase in search engine reputation is admittedly arbitrary, however. While some blogs reap the benefits of a custom domain and notice more reader activity, other blogs do not experience this to such an extent. Regardless, looking at this from a practical standpoint, your blog will stand out in the search results more with a custom domain. Some believe that your own domain makes the blog more interesting and unique, and they may be more liable to visit your website when presented to them in the search results.

Original Content

Posting original, useful content is one of the most important things you can do for your SEO. Remember that Google wants to provide their users with the most pertinent and useful search results, which is exactly why you should strive to provide just that. If it is painfully obvious that you are simply copying the content of other blogs, the harsh reality is that your blog is not going to get very far. Let us say that consumers are searching for a solution to a ceiling leak. If your blog explains how to solve the problem in a cogent, original manner, it is safe to presume that your blog is going to be shared among readers. More sharing inevitably translates to a higher ranking in Google – this is why the type of content you produce is so important.

Blog Post Optimization

This should be a given, but you would be surprised at the lack of cognizance on the importance of the structure and style of your blog posts. To elucidate, this entails the incorporation of strategic paragraphs, headings for those paragraphs, bullet points (where applicable), and hyperlinking keywords or phrases to your other articles. Take a look at several prominent blogs, and you will quickly find that they use most if not all of the aforementioned elements. Noticing simple elements such as these in popular blogs will help you go a long way in your efforts to make your blog success-worthy. The SEO benefits may not be apparent at first, but boosting the appealing factors of your blog will increase the likelihood that others share your blog. Remember, the more your blog is shared, the higher the ranking of your blog in the search results.

Create Blog Post Titles Rich in Keywords

Each of the titles for your articles should have a more specific name for the post. This is because a vague title such as "A Few Recommendations of Mine" are too vague and do not give the readers any idea of what content the post contains in the search results. Potential readers are not searching for vague phrases such as these, anyway. Create titles for your articles that you think consumers are most apt to search for such as "How to Replace a Flat Tire." This will increase the visibility of your said blog post to the readers perusing the search results. To further accentuate the prominence of your blog titles, consider the following:

- **Use numbers where applicable in your titles:** This is recommended for the simple fact that readers are naturally drawn to titles that have a number in them such as "50 Ways to Make Money" as opposed to its duller counterpart "Ways to Make Money."
- **The first few words of your title are the most important:** The first few words of blog titles are more heavily weighted by search engines, so it would be wise to make them count. An example could be "Google Blogger: A Step by Step Guide." Remember: The keywords should be kept as close to the front of the title as possible.
- **Be descriptive and use adjectives:** Which group of words sounds more captivating to you? "Incredible, fascinating, and remarkable," or "great, cool, and fine?" Give your titles a little more pizzazz, and your readers will have a higher propensity of clicking the link to see what all the fuss is about.

Work On Obtaining Backlinks

This is especially important. For the uninitiated, backlinks are simply links on other websites that redirect to your website or blog. The more high-quality backlinks you have, the higher ranked your website will be in the results pages of search engines such as Google. As part of their criteria for determining the relevance of websites, search engines assess the number of *quality* backlinks websites have. Therefore, you should not simply be bent on obtaining as many backlinks as possible because search engines give more credit to websites that have the most quality backlinks. This means you should never buy backlinks, as they are not reliable and will likely be caught on by Google. The backlinks should also be coming from websites that are as relevant and popular as possible, as this will increase the quality of the said backlinks. The best way to go about this is to guest-post on blogs related to your niche and to continue writing high-quality articles.

Internal Links

Internal links are the links on your website that lead to other pages on your blog. Do not neglect hyperlinking certain words or phrases in your articles to other articles. This is not only for the sake of reader convenience, but for increasing the Google PageRank of the said pages. By building up the internal links on your website, this makes it easier for the search engines to crawl your pages – the implication being that your pages are more likely to turn up in the search results. By hyperlinking relevant keywords to other articles, those pages will be more relevant to the said keywords and phrases. For this reason, the blogger should ensure that the hyperlinked words are not simply "here" or other vague words, but more pertinent keywords that describe the content in the link such as "here are a few reasons to start blogging" or "SEO tips."

Say Goodbye to Writer's Block

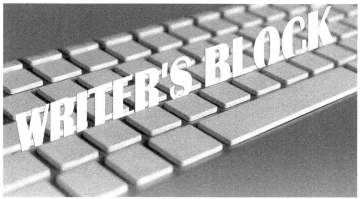

The inevitable writer's block has stricken you, and you have run out of ideas for new content. What should you do? The longer you wait, the more impatient your readers become. They are waiting on you to release your next post; you must post something before you begin losing your readers! This runs through the mind of many bloggers, and we are all bound to encounter writer's block at one point or another. It is a frustrating time for many and can be discouraging to aspiring bloggers. Do not allow this to cause you to quit blogging, however, because even the most experienced writers will encounter a dry spell every once in a while. So what do seasoned bloggers do when they are not sure what to write about? They get creative and find ways to rekindle their creativity, of course. Here are a few tips and tricks for overcoming this hurdle when it arises so you can get back to pumping out fresh content.

Consider Your Audience

This should be one of the first things to assess when the creative well has dried up. You are thinking about your audience, are you not? If you have not already, consider the demographics of your readers. Place yourself in the shoes of your audience. What would *they* want you to write about? If you were an avid reader of your blog, what kind of information would you need or want? Surely you have had a desire for a post on a specific topic from another blog, so try replicating this thought process, only with your own blog instead. You may even consider mentally changing your audience so as to clarify your purpose.

Get Ideas from Your Readers

Who better to consult than the audience itself? In this case, you can let them do the heavy thinking for you. After all, the readers themselves will feel empowered upon noticing that you are taking some of their advice. Consider perusing the comments of your articles and seeing if any of them suggest ideas for new posts. If not, perhaps you could write a post asking your readers what they want you to write about. An alternative method to this is implement a plugin or button that reads "suggest a blog post," where readers can more directly offer input on what you should write about. Of course, you may not have a following sufficient enough to use this method. In that case, it would be preferable to use the other methods of generating content ideas in this chapter and returning to this option once you have amassed enough readers.

See What Others are Blogging About

Do what you must to keep your blog afloat, right? Keep up with your competition; see the content they are writing that seems to compel their readers to return. In fact, there is a good chance that this is what your competitors are doing as well. Everyone encounters the inevitable dry spell at some point. That is not to say that you should allow it to be obvious that you are getting your ideas from another source. Stealing others' content outright could get you in trouble with not only your competitors but Google as well. You can, however, take into consideration what other experts are blogging about. Then, you can incorporate your own twist and bring something fresh to your audience. For example, if your niche is in website design and you see a blogger with a post on how to use a certain program, you could make a post on how to go about that with an alternative program. The possibilities are endless.

Review a Product/Service in Your Niche

Reviewing a product or a service makes for a great topic for you to blog about. Have you purchased or tried something recently and would like to voice your opinion about it? Blog about it! As long as the said product or service is within the realms of your niche, anything is fair game. This is because when you review something that is relevant to your niche, your audience is bound to be interested to hear what you have to say. In fact, it would be wise to stray from reviewing anything that is not pertinent to the theme of your blog. Doing so will make you appear too self-serving, confuse readers, and ultimately cause you to lose some readers. If the product or service has left an indelibly positive impression on you, then this would be the perfect opportunity to incorporate affiliate links.

Write a How-To Series

After all, you are the go-to expert of your blog's niche, are you not? Since your audience is clearly interested in your niche, then there is bound to be something that they would like to learn about in your niche. This could go any number of ways; get creative with this one. Do you blog about your experiences with gardening and some tips and tricks you have learned along the way? Create a series of blog posts detailing how to grow certain vegetables, perhaps, and what pitfalls to avoid. Your readers will be refreshed to see a how-to series that is not blatantly deriving its ideas from other sources, and your blog will likely be recommended by them provided the content is quality. This is also a great method for churning out multiple blog posts rather than struggling to come up with just one post.

Blog about Current Events

If you are not already, keep up to date with information pertaining to your niche. There is no reason that you should not already be doing so; after all, you did choose the niche. Assume that you are blogging somewhere in the automobile niche. If, for example, an automobile manufacturer makes a controversial decision, this would be the perfect opportunity for you to write a blog post on your thoughts about it. In such a case, readers would undoubtedly be curious to hear what you have to say – especially when the more prominent and controversial any given event is. A general rule of thumb when it comes to blogging about current events is this: As long as it relates to your blog in some way, there is no reason you should not go ahead and write a post on it.

Take a Break Outside

Here is a piece of advice you may not have expected: Step away from the computer and take a break outside. Nature sparks creativity; this is common knowledge that seems to be overlooked by many for some reason. When all else fails in an attempt to find something to blog about, this is an indication that it is time for you to free yourself from the writing table and to clear your mind. The ideas may be locked in the back of your head, and the serenity of the outdoors could be just what you need to reel out these ideas. Embrace nature, even if only briefly, and you may find yourself pleased with what you are inspired to write about.

Work Smarter, Not Harder

Sometimes, the effort of blogging seems too great to be worth the payback, but it does not have to be that way. To be the owner of a successful blog, all the correct factors have to fall into place. This includes quality articles, building an online presence, search engine optimization, social media marketing, and much more. It is not easy work, but not everything you do in your efforts to run a successful blog has to be incredibly convoluted or difficult. Blogging is not all about SEO, social networking, and clever titles. There is more to it than just the traditionally recommended tips and tricks you commonly hear. Make the correct moves, and everything will begin falling into place eventually. The following are simply a few simple tips to bear in mind when starting up a blog so as to make your life easier.

Choose a Niche Propelled by Passion

Make no mistake, it is important to ensure that the niche you are considering has demand and is not oversaturated. However, you do not want to write about something you are disinterested in. This only makes it all the more difficult for you to write new posts and remain motivated to continue blogging – not to mention the additional research required on your part! If not a niche you are passionate about, then opt for a subject area you are knowledgeable about. Choosing a topic that exhibits both apathy and ignorance on your end is the first step towards failure. If you are going to spend hours on the keyboard working hard, it might as well be about something you enjoy or can easily discourse at great length.

Less is More

Subject your blog to the scrutiny of not only yourself but others as well. Posit the question: Is every element seen absolutely needed? If not, then it is time to reconsider how you construct your blog's web pages. Every element on your blog needs to either be beneficial to readers in some way or nudging the users toward something you want them to do – such as signing up for your newsletter or sharing one or more of your blog posts. Useless clutter may not be apparent at first, but take the time to investigate whether everything is being used (such as the search bar) and what you can do without. After all, you do want your readers to focus on your content and not the junk that they probably will not use on the sidebar, do you not? Simplicity is the key here.

Do Not Forget the Subheadings

The emphasis of the article's title is always stressed, but what about its lesser known subordinate? Something that is easy to forget is the incorporation of subheadings in your blog posts. Take a look at a few reasonably popular blogs, and you will quickly notice that most if not all of them use subheadings at one point or another – and for good reason, too. Subheadings keep the readers from becoming bored too easily and is more convenient for the readers in that they can peruse the articles much more smoothly. Subheadings will indubitably boost audience retention rates – something worth keeping in mind to help ensure your blogging efforts are not in vain.

Place Social Media Buttons Strategically

It has already been established that all bloggers should have social media to boost traffic to their websites, but why not be smart about this? At the bottom of every blog post, place a few social media buttons that enable the readers to share your post. What this would look like is a pop-up window upon clicking one of the buttons, which then prompts readers to login with their info in order to share the post with their friends. This is quite the strategic move for the simple fact that readers who finish reading your post will have a higher propensity for being interested by your writing. Interested readers are much more likely to share your content: Why not make it that much easier for them and boost your blog's exposure as well?

Be Strategic with Your Newsletter

This is the same concept as placing your social media share buttons at the bottom of every blog post. If you plan to have a newsletter, which you should, then it would be most effective to place the option to sign up at the bottom of every article. In the hypothetical "box," ask the reader something along the lines of "Like what you see?" Then, make your call to action by inviting them to join the many readers who have subscribed to your newsletter. Do not forget to offer a free eBook as incentive for signing up. This is the most effective method of persuading your audience to subscribe to your newsletter, because once again, it is usually only the interested readers who actually make it to the bottom of your articles.

Embed the Occasional YouTube Video

Embedding videos on your blog posts attract viewership from both search engines and YouTube itself. Of course, this does not mean you should redirect all your focus to YouTube now, but it would be beneficial to post the occasional YouTube video in conjunction with your blog post. Videos can breathe a new life into your posts and provide a refreshing mix for readers. Much of what you wrote can be expounded upon in a quick, 2 minute video. In fact, it could even go the other way around and your video could be the meat of the content instead. Ensure that the video is embedded near the top of your blog post so that readers do not miss out on it.

Be Transparent

Let your audience get to know you as a person. This might not bode well for reserved writers, but it is essential for establishing a connection with your audience. Create an "about me" page that details who you are and your story. Readers are more likely to trust you and more people will be able to relate to you as a result. Be honest and upfront with the purpose of your blog, and thank your readers for taking the time to read your about section. Also consider uploading a picture of yourself on your about section to not only increase your credibility, but to allow your audience to see you as a person and not just another blogger. Many prominent bloggers have a picture of themselves on both the home page and about section – something worth keeping in mind.

Dangerous Blogging Mistakes to Avoid

Blogging has the potential to take you where you want it to if you follow the correct steps. However, the pitfalls that aspiring bloggers should steer clear of have not yet been addressed. These said pitfalls can be the factors that turn off your audience and cause you to lose potential readership. Do not let that happen to you. This chapter is focused on helping you evade the common mistakes of many novice bloggers so as to avoid any potential setbacks in the future. For example, if there is something you failed to do or did incorrectly in every blog post only to find this out much later, it would likely be difficult and time-consuming to go back and rectify all instances of the error. Some of what will be discussed may sound obvious, but you would be surprised at the lack of cognizance on certain matters. Regardless, do stray from committing any of the following mistakes, and you and your blog should be fine.

Bombarding Readers with Advertisements

You want to make money from your hard work blogging – that much is understandable. What is not acceptable, however, is the implementation of so many advertisements that your readers are infuriated and leave your blog, never to return again. And rightfully so! When the advertisements overshadow the content of the blog, why would readers want to stay? Too often, bloggers will become "advertisement-happy" in an attempt to milk as much money as possible, but this would be completely counterproductive. This only works against them in the end, and there are better methods of profiting from your blog as will be covered in the upcoming chapter: Monetization Tactics.

Failing to Properly Hyperlink Words

What is meant by this is hyperlinking something along the lines of "For additional information pertaining to this matter, click here." Rather than hyperlinking "click here," it would be much more effective to hyperlink words that are actually relevant to the content in the link. Something more effective would look similar to "We can help you gather information on the most effective SEO tips." Do you see how much more visually appealing and descriptive the latter is? The reader is more likely to click the latter hyperlink, especially if that person is just skimming through the article. In any case, it has already been covered that hyperlinking words relevant to the content within the link will boost SEO, so there is no reason this should not already be in practice.

Unintentional Plagiarism

Regrettably, this must be addressed for the simple fact that beginner bloggers have a propensity for unintentionally committing plagiarism. This is usually the case when a blogger searches an image on Google and uses that image without a second thought. Even if the blogger acknowledges the source of the image, this does not extricate the person from plagiarism. In fact, the U.S. Copyright Office states here that "Acknowledging the source of the copyrighted material does not substitute for obtaining permission." So, what should you do if you cannot pull an image found on Google? You resort to free stock images or royalty-free photos, of course. Royalty free images are incredibly useful and serve a wide variety of purposes: Use them.

Inconsistent Writing

You must establish a firmly entrenched schedule in when you choose to publish your next blog post. Nothing will throw off an audience more than an inconsistency in your writing. This does not mean you should proceed with the mentality "I'll just make up a few posts this week since I've promised my readers X number of posts per week." Choose a schedule that you think you can handle and stick to it. Putting off the blog post on the day you have promised your readers will bring you into disrepute in the eyes of your readers. Here is the takeaway: Stay consistent in both the quality of your writing *and* the frequency you publish your posts. This can go a long way in building an audience and retaining viewership.

Not Engaging with Your Audience

Too often, bloggers will neglect their readers in the comments section and cause readers to feel ignored. New bloggers should have no excuse for not responding to most if not all of the comments left behind on their posts. This builds a stronger relationship with your readers and they will consequently feel more connected to you. Even prominent bloggers will respond to at least *some* of the earliest comments as an indication that they do read the readers' comments. There is a reason that they do so; replying to someone's comment will leave an indelible impression on some and increases the likelihood that the blogger is remembered. Do not leave a generic "I agree with you" comment, but actually take the time to thoughtfully respond. This way, people will not forget you so easily.

Lack of Collaboration with Other Bloggers

Find bloggers in your niche and reach out to them for collaboration in the hopes of promoting each other. Perhaps you are skeptical of doing so, because they are your competitors, after all. This would be a dire mistake, however, and you cannot expect to go this alone forever. There is always enough business to go around, and you cannot remain stuck in the "all for me" mentality. One way to collaborate with other bloggers would be to mutually agree to promote each other's blogs on the sidebars of your blogs. By cooperating with your competitors, everyone benefits from increased visibility and ultimately what everyone wants: traffic. Try grouping your efforts together so that you can all be successful rather than embarking the blogging journey alone.

Focusing Only on Writing

Content is indeed king, but the writer has to do much more than that if he or she has hopes of ever amassing traffic for the website. With this mentality, the blogger will wind up writing post after post only to end up frustrated at the lack of viewership and ultimately give up. It is easy for the aspiring blogger to focus solely on the writing aspect of running a blog; after all, it is one of the main aspects of a blog. However, you cannot afford to forget about all the other factors that must fall into place for the blog to take off: social media, collaboration with other bloggers, SEO, reader engagement, newsletter setup, the proper niche, etc.

Monetization Tactics

      We have finally arrived to the final chapter that details one of the many driving factors of running a blog: monetization. Assume you have finally garnered a decent source of traffic for your blog. Your content could be original, high quality, and praised by avid readers of your blog. Now what? You do not want all your effort and hard work to go to waste, do you? That is where this chapter comes into play. There are several different monetization methods at the blogger's disposal, so this should not be a problem on your end. Certain monetization tactics are going to be more profitable than others, but the difficulty in implementing these monetization strategies vary from method to method. Some only become worth the time and effort once you have amassed enough of a following, so your judgment will be required on that end. Regardless, here are some obvious (and not so obvious) monetization strategies you will undoubtedly want to pursue.

Advertisements

      First, we will address the most popular and conspicuous monetization method for not just blogging but a variety of online services. Sign up for a provider such as Google AdSense, and you will be able to place ads relevant to the content of your blog on the sides. Of course, it should be iterated that you must stray from bombarding your blog with ads in hopes of boosting revenue, as this will negatively impact readership and drive away visitors. While money can be made from impression of the ads, the bulk of the revenue comes from the ads' click-through rate (CTR). This requires a high source of traffic, so do not expect to become affluent with ads and a modest source of traffic. On the flip side, this is also the least time consuming monetization method as you can simply set the ads and forget about it.

Affiliate Marketing

This is another common revenue model for bloggers to resort to and can be lucrative if executed properly. Whenever someone purchases that product after clicking your affiliate link, you receive a commission. Percentages of the sale price vary, however, depending on the affiliate network and the product. If you have left a positive review on a product pertinent to your niche, this is the quintessential opportunity to implement an affiliate link. Another opportunity to incorporate your affiliate link is if you were to make a blog post on "the best type of X," x being something relevant to your niche. For example, if you run a video game themed blog, you could post an article titled "What are the best action games this year?" At the end of the post, you could then introduce affiliate links for the products. This could go any number of ways, and the options are yours for the choosing.

Sell Your Own Products

When a blogger promotes his or her own products, it has the tendency to establish that blogger as an expert in that niche. After all, running a blog is all about driving traffic to that website. Admittedly, creating your own products is no easy feat, especially for new bloggers with limited resources. Digital content is always a good place to start; you can never go wrong with this type of product offering. "What kind of products should I sell?" you might ask. That entirely depends on your niche and where your strength lies. Are your blogging about something musically related? If you have the talent, then this is the perfect opportunity to create instrumentals through a musical program and promote those tunes through the mediums you offer them. Whatever it is you have to offer, promoting your own products through your blog also brings along the perks of long-term SEO benefits.

Sponsored Advertising

Keep this monetization method in mind for when you have a considerable source of traffic. Sponsored advertising is similar to the traditional advertising model but requires that the blogger already be somewhat prominent. With this monetization method, advertisers will naturally find your blog assuming that it is well known enough. Some advertisers want their exposure to be on your social media, while others would like you to promote them through your blog. Obviously, the downside is that you would be waiting in the hopes of the advertisers contacting you. Alternatively, you could pitch them and cross your fingers for a positive response. When your blog takes off, you may consider creating an advertising page exclusively for sponsors interested in purchasing advertising packages. In the page, you could outline the prices and what you have to offer as well as your blog's demographics and statistics. To maximize your chances of the sponsors contacting you, make the advertising page as straightforward as possible.

Freelance Write

While this is not a direct method of monetization from your blog, the blog itself could help pave the way for future freelance writing. Even if your blog is not profiting from heaps of cash or seeing high volumes of traffic, it is nonetheless a great item to add to your portfolio of work. You never know what kind of future opportunities will be open to you, as your blog will be a representation of your ability to write. What would be most opportune is if you came across work requiring freelance writing that relates to your niche. With the presentation of your (professional, sleek, and long-term) blog, that would make you a shoe-in for that particular work.

Donate Button

Here is one more idea for monetizing your blog: Consider implementing a "donate" button on the sidebar of your blog so that your readers can offer a token of appreciation for your hard work. This is not something to feel guilty about, because you are simply offering readers the opportunity to support you for your hard work. You do provide information for others, so you probably deserve it! When you truly provide high quality content on a regular basis and interact with readers in the comments section, readers cannot help but want to reciprocate your efforts. Add the donate button; provided you have a moderate source of traffic and the aforementioned criteria, you can expect to be directly rewarded by the avid readers of your blog for your efforts.

Closing Words

      Running a successful blog is no easy feat, but nothing worth it is ever easy, right? The technical aspects of blogging are volatile, and you will need to keep up with said technical aspects as a blogger to keep your website up to date. There are many things to consider when jumping into the land of blogging, but you should now have a clearer understanding of how to proceed after reading this eBook. From choosing a niche and marketing your blog to monetization and overcoming writer's block, there is bound to be something here that you can refer back to in the future! Hopefully, you have gained something from this eBook and will use these tips in your quest for passive income with blogging. Good luck with your blogging efforts and may luck happen to shine upon you!

If you have found my work to be useful to you in any way, please feel free to leave a review.